This book belongs to _____

A Kid's Guide to Boston's

Freedom Trail

© 1991 by
Jane and Gary Ferguson
Lita and Mike Ebersole
illustrated by
Marie Miller

Produced by GCBA Publishing
P.O. Box 292
Grand Canyon, Arizona 86023

printed on recycled paper

Boston Common

The Freedom Trail begins at Boston Common, America's oldest public park. A group of colonists known as the Puritans bought this land from W. Blackstone in 1634. They called it a "common land" because people shared it, mostly for grazing cattle.

Many amazing things have happened at Boston Common. Pirates were hung here. British troops camped here during the Revolutionary War. For a time, people would even dump their garbage here. Draw a picture of what you see happening - or what you think might happen - on the Common today.

FREEDOM TRAIL TIC-TAC-TOE

(a brick pattern)

(a sign)

(a window pattern)

(a window pattern)

As you walk the Freedom Trail, look carefully for each of the above items. Whenever you spot one, mark the appropriate square with the first letter of your name. Mark 3 in a row — across, up and down, or diagonal — and you've got a TIC-TAC-TOE! (If 2 or more of you are playing, squares are marked by the first person to see each item.)

For many years, Old South Meeting House was the largest building in Boston. It often hosted large crowds of colonists, who came together to protest things they did not like about British rule. (On the night of the Boston Tea Party in 1773, 5,000 people gathered here!) Today Old South Meeting House is still a place where people gather—to learn history, and to see plays, lectures, and concerts. Can you fill this picture with people?

Old State House
built 1713

Old South Meeting House
built 1729

If you look closely at the brick buildings along the Freedom Trail, you'll see that the bricks are laid in different patterns. Bricks laying flat on their sides like this ▭ ▭ are called stretchers. If just the end shows ▢▢▢, we call these headers. And bricks standing up like this ▯▯▯ are known as soldiers. Make up your own brick patterns and draw them below.

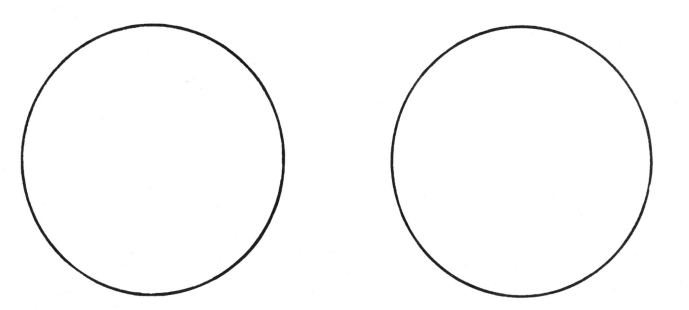

John Adams, second president of the United States, once said that America's Independence was born at Old State House. He said this because it was here that elected officials from throughout the colony first gathered to complain about what they thought were unfair British laws and taxes. These taxes were one of the things that led the colonists to fight for independence.

Old State House is also where the people of Boston first heard a reading of the Declaration of Independence. The Declaration of Independence is still read here every 4th of July.

Figures of many animals can be seen along or near the Freedom Trail. A wooden lion and a unicorn stand for the powers of British Royalty. Nearby is an American eagle with a wingspan of more than 8 feet. A black, metal cow sits on top of an old market. And finally, there's a 250-year-old copper grasshopper with glass eyes! Can you find these members of the "Freedom Trail Zoo" hidden in the picture above?

Nowhere has the idea of free speech been more celebrated than on the second floor of Faneuil Hall. Colonists gathered here to challenge British laws that seemed unfair to them. Issues like slavery, women's rights and the Vietnam War have also been debated.

Today Faneuil Hall is still a place for free expression. Is there something you feel strongly about? What would you want to say about this subject to people gathered at Faneuil Hall?

_____

_____

_____

_____

_____

What Is It?

Below are some common objects from early New England. Can you guess what they are? What objects in your house might be hard for people to identify 200 years from now?

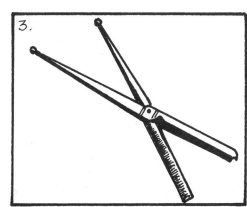

1. mortar and pestle (Used to grind dried herbs and spices as well as coarse sugar and salt.)

2. foot warmer (Hot coals were placed inside. Popular in many churches.)

3. curling iron (For wigs. Curls could be added by heating the iron, and then clamping it around moist wig hair.)

4. ice skates

5. egg beater

6. bed wrench (Early beds had no springs. Instead, a long rope was threaded back and forth through holes in the frame, and a mattress placed on top. When the rope sagged, this wrench tightened it.)

Sign Language

sailor's hotel

tavern

Because not everyone in early Boston could read, shopkeepers advertised their businesses with signs like these. Look for these signs along the Freedom Trail. What other shop signs can you come up with? Draw them below.

baked beans

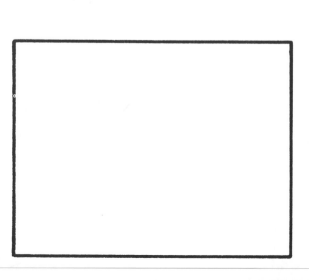

Paul Revere House - Built c.1680

    The Paul Revere House is just as interesting on the outside as it is on the inside. See how the second story hangs out over the front door? That kind of construction, called "overhang", is a style that dates back more than 500 years! The fact that the Revere House was built with wood is a good clue to how old it really is. Why do you think so many of the newer buildings along the Freedom Trail were built with bricks instead of wood?

    How is your home like the Revere House? How is it different?

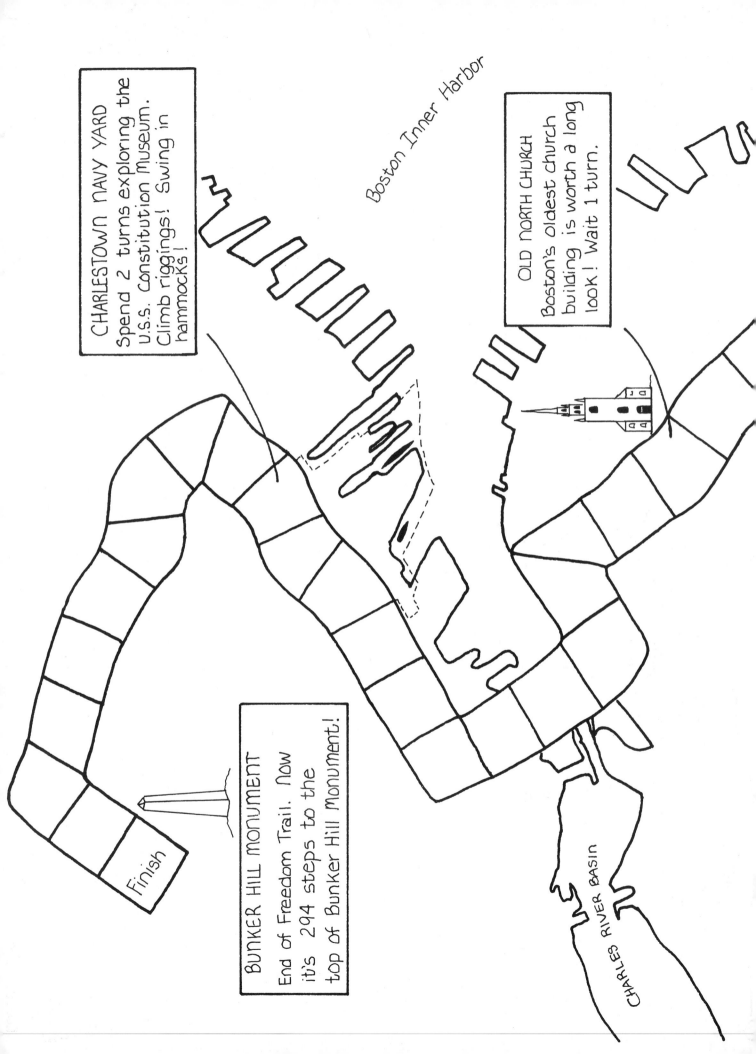

CHARLESTOWN NAVY YARD

Spend 2 turns exploring the U.S.S. Constitution museum. Climb riggings! Swing in hammocks!

Boston Inner Harbor

OLD NORTH CHURCH

Boston's oldest church building is worth a long look! Wait 1 turn.

BUNKER HILL MONUMENT

End of Freedom Trail. Now it's 294 steps to the top of Bunker Hill Monument!

Finish

CHARLES RIVER BASIN

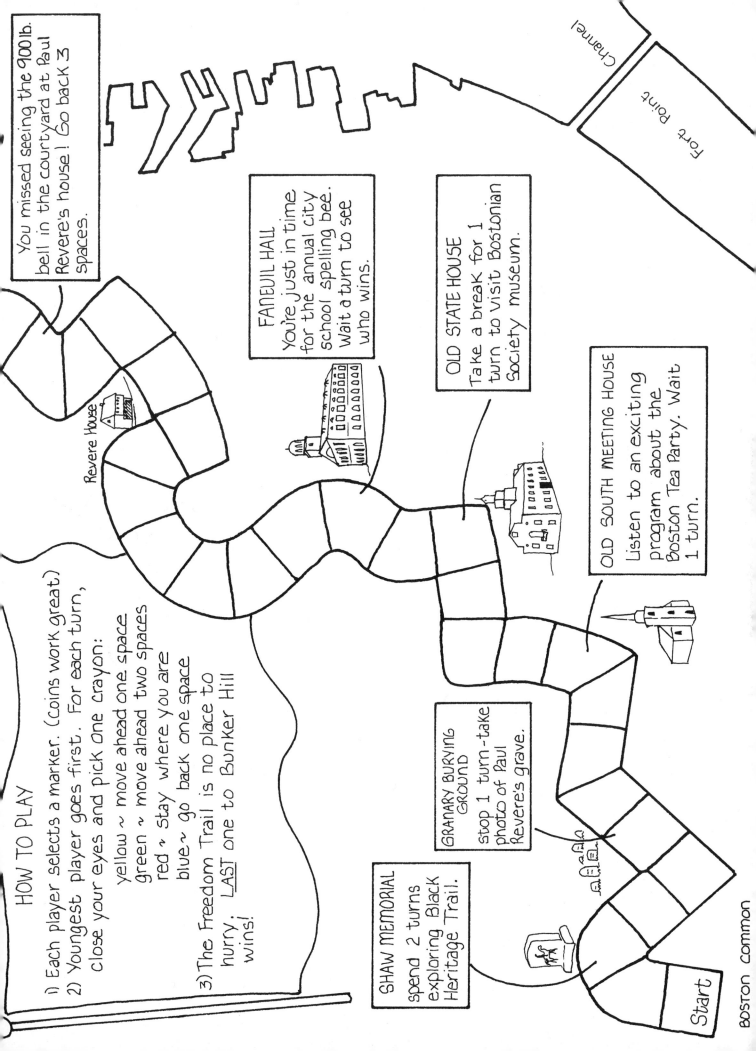

HOW TO PLAY

1) Each player selects a marker. (coins work great)
2) Youngest player goes first. For each turn, close your eyes and pick one crayon:

   yellow ~ move ahead one space
   green ~ move ahead two spaces
   red ~ stay where you are
   blue ~ go back one space

3) The Freedom Trail is no place to hurry. <u>LAST</u> one to Bunker Hill wins!

You missed seeing the 900 lb. bell in the courtyard at Paul Revere's house! Go back 3 spaces.

Revere House

FANEUIL HALL
You're just in time for the annual city school spelling bee. Wait a turn to see who wins.

OLD STATE HOUSE
Take a break for 1 turn to visit Bostonian Society museum.

OLD SOUTH MEETING HOUSE
Listen to an exciting program about the Boston Tea Party. Wait 1 turn.

SHAW MEMORIAL
spend 2 turns exploring Black Heritage Trail.

GRANARY BURYING GROUND
stop 1 turn – take photo of Paul Revere's grave.

Fort Point

Channel

Start

Boston Common

It's almost midnight on April 18TH, 1775. Paul Revere's friends have rowed him across the Charles River to Charlestown; there he has borrowed a horse. Now he must make his famous ride to Lexington to warn John Hancock and Samuel Adams that the British are coming. Can you help him find his way?

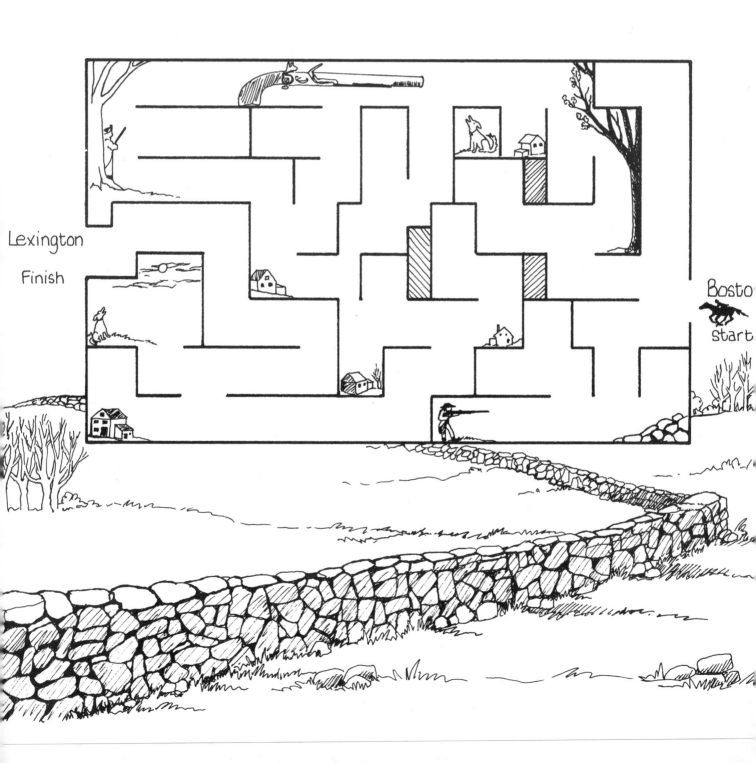

The history of Old North Church is an exciting one! On the night of April 18th, 1775, Robert Newman climbed 15 stories, lit two lanterns, and hung them in the steeple. This was a secret signal that meant British soldiers were moving across the Charles River toward Cambridge. From there, these soldiers would begin marching to Concord in an effort to capture guns and ammunition from the colonists.

Sunday services are still held in Old North Church, as they have been since 1723.

Streets of Boston

ACROSS

1. Street named for a type of waterway dug here in the 1640's; water used to power machinery and transport goods.
2. Provided Boston residents with fresh water for 200 years.
3. Street renamed in honor of a famous Revolutionary War general-later, first president.
5. Takes its name from a large triple-peaked hill once found on this peninsula. (Clue: 3-h-e + ⋀⋀-u-ain)
7. The 1ˢᵗ English settler in what is now downtown Boston.
(Clue: his name can be found on another page.)

DOWN

4. Born in 1763, he became one of Boston's greatest architects. (Clue: 🐏-l+f+ 📏)
6. Named in honor of a great Boston-born inventor.
8. A building where you go to learn. The first one of these in America, open to children free of charge, was built in 1635.

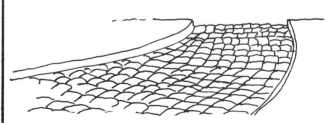

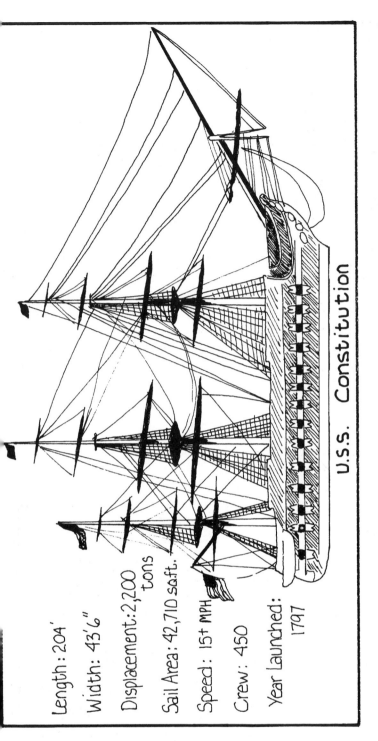

Length: 204'
Width: 43' 6"
Displacement: 2,200 tons
Sail Area: 42,710 sq.ft.
Speed: 15+ MPH
Crew: 450
Year Launched: 1797

U.S.S. Constitution

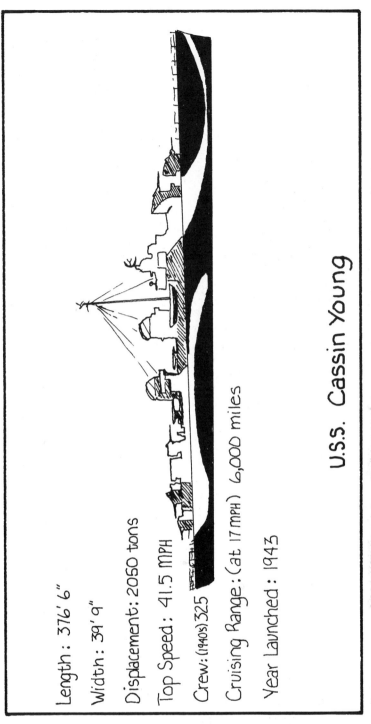

Length: 376' 6"
Width: 39' 9"
Displacement: 2050 tons
Top Speed: 41.5 MPH
Crew: (1940s) 325
Cruising Range: (at 17 MPH) 6,000 miles
Year Launched: 1943

U.S.S. Cassin Young

The Charlestown Navy Yard has cared for the ships of the U.S. Navy since 1801. Work began in the days of wooden sailing ships armed with cannon, and continued through the building of steel ships equipped with radar, sonar, and torpedos. During World War II, as many as 50,000 men and women worked at the Charlestown Navy Yard.

Bunker Hill Monument marks the place where the first major battle of the American Revolution was fought in 1775. If you were to fight a battle, this hill would be important because it provides good views of the city of Boston and its harbor.

The next spring, George Washington and his soldiers placed cannon on a high bluff of land to the southeast called Dorchester Heights. (Many of those cannon had been pulled by oxen from 300 miles away!) Those cannon made it very hard for the British to bring troops and supplies into the harbor. A few days later the British sailed out of Boston, never to return.

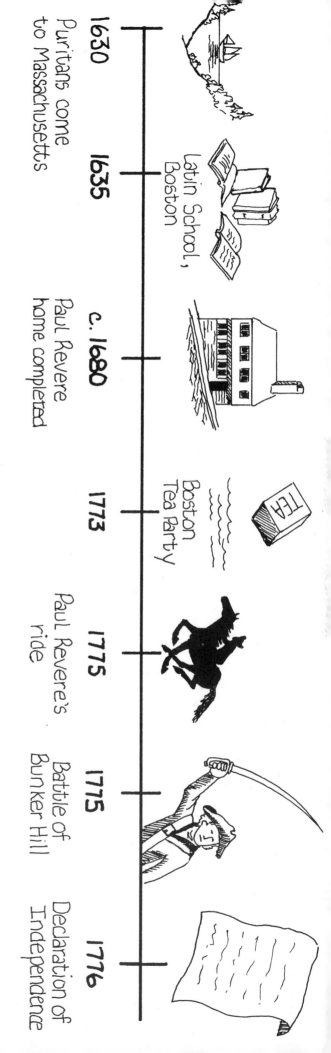

One of the best ways to understand history is by making something called a time line. Starting with the year you were born, use the important events in your life to create a time line below.

1630	1635	c.1680	1773	1775	1775	1776
Puritans come to Massachusetts	Latin School, Boston	Paul Revere's home completed	Boston Tea Party	Paul Revere's ride	Battle of Bunker Hill	Declaration of Independence

_____
(year you were born)

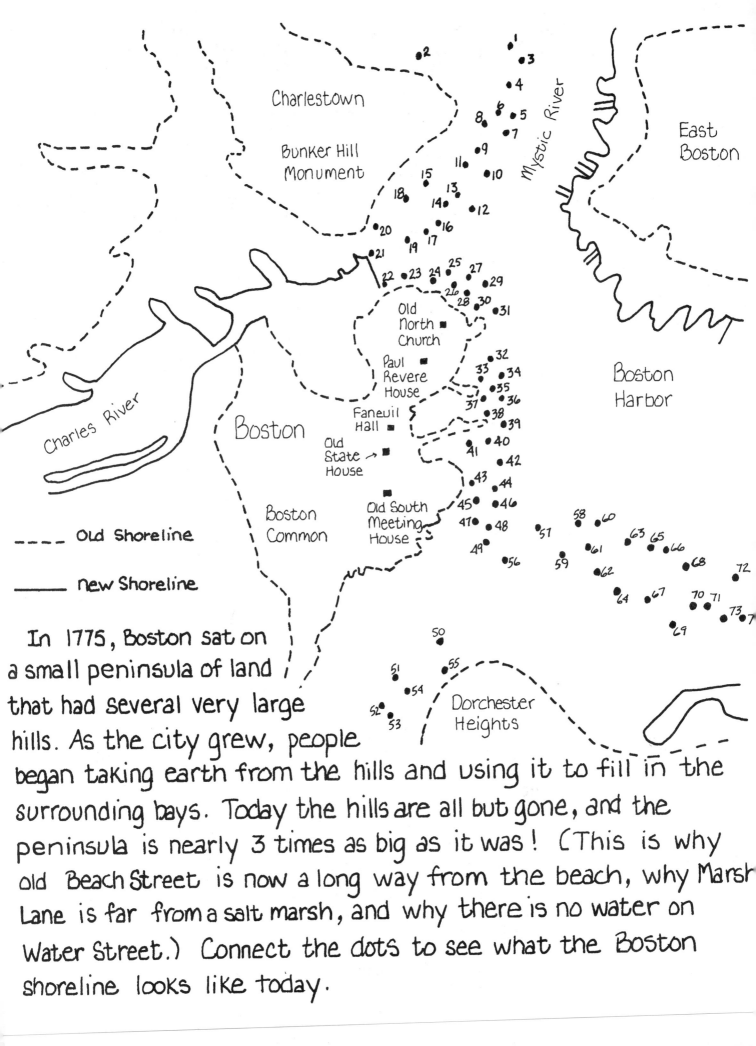

Charlestown

Bunker Hill Monument

Mystic River

East Boston

Old North Church

Paul Revere House

Faneuil Hall

Boston

Charles River

Old State House

Boston Harbor

Old South Meeting House

Boston Common

- - - - Old Shoreline

———— New Shoreline

Dorchester Heights

In 1775, Boston sat on a small peninsula of land that had several very large hills. As the city grew, people began taking earth from the hills and using it to fill in the surrounding bays. Today the hills are all but gone, and the peninsula is nearly 3 times as big as it was! (This is why old Beach Street is now a long way from the beach, why Marsh Lane is far from a salt marsh, and why there is no water on Water Street.) Connect the dots to see what the Boston shoreline looks like today.

What's Wrong?

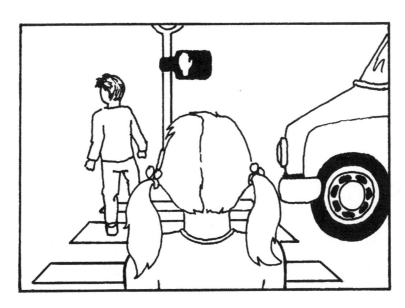

The Freedom Trail needs your help if it is to remain such a special place. The grave markers in the Granary, King's Chapel, and Copp's Hill burial grounds are very fragile. Even making headstone "rubbings" can harm them. Also, try your best to Keep the trail free from litter. And, oh yes! Be VERY careful crossing busy streets.

Visitors wanting to learn more about the Freedom Trail can go on tours with National Park Service rangers. What if you were a Park Service ranger here? Write down some questions visitors might ask you. _____

_____

The year is 1798. You are a sailor heading out to sea on the U.S.S. Constitution. Captain Nicholson says you can bring no more personal belongings than will fit into a single duffle bag. What would you pack?

_____
_____
_____

In 1860, Henry Wadsworth Longfellow wrote a poem about Paul Revere riding to warn patriot leaders that the British were coming. The poem begins like this:

"Listen, my children, and you shall hear
Of the midnight ride of Paul Revere,"

But Paul Revere was not the only messenger. William Dawes and Samuel Prescott were among the others who rode that night. Can you write a poem about one of these men?

SPEEDY BOSTON BAKED BEANS

Microwave, covered, on high for 4 minutes:

2 slices bacon, cut into pieces

1 small onion, chopped

Add:

1 31 oz. can of plain pork and beans

¼ cup of molasses

¼ cup Ketchup

1 tablespoon mustard

Mix well, then:

Microwave, covered, on high for three minutes, then on medium-low for twelve minutes.

Boston has a very long history of eating baked beans. In fact, people have long referred to Boston as "Bean Town". Some historians think that colonists first learned about baked beans from local Indians, who cooked them in pits with bear fat and maple syrup. Others, though, think that sea captains brought back the recipe from Spain or North Africa.

While the above recipe is quick, traditional baked beans took many hours to prepare.

Did You Know That...

1. many of the grave markers in the Granary Burying Ground have been moved? (In other words, "the stones don't match the bones!")

2. colonists declared lobster to be trash food, fit only for prisoners and dogs?

3. each year British soldiers used tons of flour to whiten their wigs and pants?

4. Beacon Hill (where the New Statehouse is) used to be as tall as the top of the New Statehouse dome?

5. angry British soldiers removed the seats from Old South Meeting House and turned it into a riding stable?

6. the Battle of Bunker Hill was actually fought on nearby Breed's Hill?

7. the U.S.S. Constitution is still a commissioned U.S. Navy ship?

8. British soldiers wore red coats so that the blood from their wounds would not show?